HOOKED ON BABY

When there's a baby in your life, you want to envelop that precious little person in every luxury you can provide. That's why Lion® Brand Yarn Company is your best choice for ultra-soft yarns. Homespun®, Microspun, Lion® Suede, Lion® Wool, and Tiffany yarns create crochet that is plush to the touch, making these popular fibers perfect for a teddy bear, a pocket blanket (with crocheted toy kitten), or a pair of fluffy bunny booties. If your wee one needs a warm cap or a cozy jacket, you'll find your design in this heartwarming collection of eleven versatile Lion® Brand designs.

Please visit www.LionBrand.com for useful information.

LION WOOL

GAUGE for 4"x 4" (10cm x 10cm)

US 8 5mm — 16 STS / 24 R

H-8 3.75mm — 12 SC / 15 R

SOLIDS

	NET		TOTAL	
	ozs	gms	yards	meters
	3	85	158	144

PRINTS

	NET		TOTAL	
	ozs	gms	yards	meters
	2¾	78	143	131

100% WOOL

TIFFANY

GAUGE for 4"x 4" (10cm x 10cm)

US 8 5mm — 24 STS / 32 R

J-10 6mm — 17 SC / 20 R

ozs	gms	yards	meters
1¾	50	137	125

100% NYLON

MICRO SPUN

GAUGE for 4"x 4" (10cm x 10cm)

US 4 3.25mm — 24 STS / 32 R

H-8 5mm — 13 SC / 16 R

ozs	gms	yards	meters
2½	70	168	154

100% MICROFIBER ACRYLIC

LION SUEDE

GAUGE for 4"x 4" (10cm x 10cm)

US 9 5.5mm — 12 STS / 19 R

J-10 6mm — 9 SC / 11 R

SOLIDS

ozs	gms	yards	meters
3	85	122	110

PRINTS

ozs	gms	yards	meters
2¾	78	111	101

100% POLYESTER*

HOMESPUN

GAUGE for 4"x 4" (10cm x 10cm)

10 6mm — 14 STS / 20 R

K-10.5 6.5mm — 10 SC / 10 R

	NET		TOTAL	
	ozs	gms	yards	meters
	6	170	185	169

ACRYLIC	POLYESTER
98%	2%

STRIPED BABY HAT

DESIGNER: KIM KOTARY

◗■□□ EASY +

Finished Size: S (M)
Finished head circumference: 15 (17)" [38 (43 cm)]

Note: Pattern is written for smaller size with changes for larger size in parentheses. When only one number is given, it applies to both sizes. To follow pattern more easily, circle all numbers pertaining to your size before beginning.

MATERIALS

■ LION BRAND® Microspun Microfiber Sport **LIGHT 3**
  Weight Yarn
  [2¹/₂ ounces, 168 yards (70 grams, 154 meters) per ball]
  Colorway 1
    1 ball #146 Fuchsia (A)
    1 ball #148 Turquoise (B)
    1 ball #194 Lime (C)
    or colors of your choice
  Colorway 2
    1 ball #100 Lily White (A)
    1 ball #098 French Vanilla (B)
    1 ball #124 Mocha (C)
    or colors of your choice
■ LION BRAND size H-8 [5 mm] crochet hook or size needed for gauge
■ LION BRAND large-eyed blunt needle
■ LION BRAND split ring marker
■ 2" [5 cm] square of cardboard

GAUGE

13 sts and 16 rows = 4"[10 cm] in sc with 2 strands of yarn held together

Note: Work with 2 strands of yarn held together throughout. Carry colors not in use loosely on WS of work.

HAT

Beg at crown, with 2 strands of A, ch 4. Sl st in first ch to form a ring. Place marker for beg of rnd. Sl marker each rnd.

Rnd 1: Ch 1, work 8 sc in ring. Sl st in beg ch to join each rnd.

Rnd 2: Ch 1, 2 sc in each sc around – 16 sc.

Rnd 3: Drop A and join 2 strands of B, ch 1, * sc in next sc, 2 sc in next sc; rep from * around – 24 sc.

Rnd 4: Ch 1, * sc in 2 sc, 2 sc in next sc; rep from * around – 32 sc.

Rnd 5: Ch 1, * sc in 3 sc, 2 sc in next sc; rep from * around – 40 sc.

Rnd 6: Drop B and join 2 strands of C, ch 1, * sc in 4 sc, 2 sc in next sc; rep from * around – 48 sts.

For Size Small
Rnd 7: Ch 1, sc in each sc around – 48 sts.

For Size Medium
Rnd 7: Ch 1, * sc in 5 sc, 2 sc in next sc; rep from * around – 56 sts.

For Both Sizes
Rnd 8: Ch 1, sc in each sc around.

Rnds 9 and 10: Drop C and join 2 strands of A, ch 1, sc in each sc around.

Rnds 11-13: Drop A and join 2 strands of B, ch 1, sc in each sc around.

Rnds 14-16: Drop B and join 2 strands of C, ch 1, sc in each sc around.

Rnds 17 and 18: Drop C and join 2 strands of A, ch 1, sc in each sc around. Fasten off.

RIGHT EAR FLAP

Row 1: Sk 6 (8) sc from center back, attach 2 strands of B with sl st in the next sc, sc in next 10 sc. Turn each row.

Row 2: Ch 1, sc in 9 sc.

Row 3: Ch 1, sc in 8 sc. Fasten off but do not cut yarn.

Row 4: Attach 2 strands of C with sl st in first st, ch 1, sc in 7 sc.

Row 5: Ch 1, sc in 6 sc.

Continued on page 21.

CROCHET TEDDY BEAR

DESIGNER: **KAREN HAY**

◼◼◼◻ INTERMEDIATE

Finished Size: 10½" [26.5 cm] long
Seated Height: 6½" [16.5 cm]

MATERIALS

◼ LION BRAND® Homespun® Textured Bulky **5** BULKY
Weight Yarn
[6 ounces, 185 yards (170 grams, 169 meters)
per skein]
1 skein #380 Fawn
or color of your choice
◼ LION BRAND® Microspun Microfiber Sport **3** LIGHT
Weight Yarn
[2½ ounces, 168 yards (70 grams, 154 meters)
per ball]
    1 ball #194 Lime
or color of your choice
◼ Small amount black worsted weight yarn
◼ LION BRAND size J-10 [6 mm] crochet hook or
size needed for gauge
◼ LION BRAND size H-8 [5 mm] crochet hook or
size needed for gauge
◼ LION BRAND split ring marker
◼ LION BRAND large-eyed blunt needle
◼ Polyester fiberfill stuffing

GAUGE

With Homespun and larger hook, 12 sc
and 14 rows = 4" [10 cm]
With Microspun and smaller hook, 16 sc = 4"
[10 cm]

STITCH EXPLANATIONS

sc2tog (sc dec): Insert hook into st and draw up a
loop. Insert hook into next st and draw up a loop.
Yarn over, draw through all 3 loops on hook.

TEDDY
HEAD AND BODY

Note: Most of the Head and Body are worked in rnds. Sl st in first sc to join each rnd. The first sc in each rnd is worked in the same st as the joining. Before beginning, reserve 2 yd [91.5 cm] of yarn for use in making the Muzzle (Rows 1-4).

Rnd 1: Begin with slipknot, leaving a 6" [15 cm] yarn tail, work 8 sc in sl st; sl st in first sc to join each rnd. After working the first rnd, pull gently on the yarn tail to close ring. Place marker for beg of rnd. Sl marker each rnd.

Rnd 2: Ch 1, 2 sc in each sc around – 16 sc.

Rnd 3: Ch 1, * sc in next sc, 2 sc in next sc; rep from * around – 24 sc.

Rnds 4 and 5: Ch 1, sc in each sc around. Drop yarn, but do not fasten off.

Shape Muzzle
Note: Muzzle is worked in rows.

Row 1: Sk 8 sc, attach reserved yarn in next sc, ch 1, sc in same sc, sc in next 7 sc – 8 sc. Turn each row.

Row 2: Ch 1, sc2tog, sc in 4 sc, sc2 tog – 6 sc.

Row 3: Ch 1, sc2tog, sc in 2 sc, sc2tog – 4 sc.

Row 4: Ch 1, (sc2tog) twice – 2 sc. Fasten off Muzzle yarn. Pick up yarn that was dropped following Rnd 5.

Rnd 6: Ch 1, sc in first 8 sc of Rnd 5, 2 sc in sc where reserved yarn was joined, work 4 sc evenly up side of Muzzle, sc in 2 sc at top of Muzzle, work 4 sc evenly down other side of Muzzle, 2 sc in last sc of Row 1 of Muzzle, sc in last 8 sc of Rnd 5 – 30 sc.

Rnds 7 and 8: Ch 1, sc in each sc around.

Rnd 9: Ch 1, sc in 4 sc, sc2tog, sc in 3 sc, * sc2tog, sc in 2 sc, sc2tog; rep from * once, sc in 3 sc, sc2tog, sc in 4 sc – 24 sc.

Rnd 10: Ch 1, * sc in next sc, sc2tog; rep from * around – 16 sc.

Rnd 11: Ch 1, * sc2tog; rep from * around – 8 sc. Stuff head.

Rnd 12: Ch 1, 2 sc in each sc around – 16 sc.

Rnd 13: Ch 1, * sc in next sc, 2 sc in next sc; rep from * around – 24 sc.

Rnd 14: Ch 1, * sc in 2 sc, 2 sc in next sc, rep from * around – 32 sc.

Continued on pages 21-22.

CROSS-FRONT BABY SWEATER

DESIGNER: **VASHTI BRAHA**

■■■□ INTERMEDIATE

Finished Sizes: 6 (12, 18, 24) months
Finished Chest: 22 (24, 25, 26)"
[56 (61, 63.5, 66) cm]
Finished Length: 11$\frac{1}{2}$ (12, 12$\frac{1}{2}$, 13)" [29 (30.5, 31.5, 33) cm]

Note: Pattern is written for smallest size with changes for larger sizes in parentheses. When only one number is given, it applies to all sizes. To follow pattern more easily, circle all numbers pertaining to your size before beginning.

MATERIALS
- ■ LION BRAND® Lion® Suede Bulky Weight Yarn
  [Solid colors: 3 ounces, 122 yards (85 grams, 110 meters); Prints: 2$\frac{3}{4}$ ounces, 111 yards (78 grams, 101 meters) per ball]
  3 (3, 4, 4) balls #140 Rose
  or color of your choice
- ■ LION BRAND crochet hook size K-10.5 [6.5 mm] or size needed for gauge
- ■ LION BRAND large-eyed blunt needle

GAUGE
10 sc and 11 rows = 4" [10 cm]

STITCH EXPLANATION
sc2tog (sc dec): Insert hook into st and draw up a loop. Insert hook into next st and draw up a loop. Yarn over, draw through all 3 loops on hook.

SWEATER
BODY
Ch 78 (82, 85, 90).

Row 1: Sc in 2nd ch from hook and in each ch across – 77 (81, 84, 89) sc. Turn.

Row 2: Ch 1, sc in each sc across. Turn each row.

Rows 3-16 (3-17, 3-18, 3-18): Rep Row 2.

Shape Fronts
Row 17 (18, 19, 19): Ch 1, sk first sc, sc in each sc to last 2 sc, sc2tog – 75 (79, 82, 87) sc.

Row 18 (19, 20, 20): Work even.

Row 19 (20, 21, 21): Repeat Row 17 (18, 19, 19) – 73 (77, 80, 85) sc.

Divide for Fronts and Back

Right Front
Row 20 (21, 22, 22): Ch 1, sk first sc, sc in next 21 (22, 23, 25) sc (leave remaining sts unworked) – 21 (22, 23, 25) sc.

Row 21 (22, 23, 23): Ch 1, sc in each sc to last 2 sc, sc2tog – 20 (21, 22, 24) sc.

Row 22 (23, 24, 24): Ch 1, sk first sc, sc in each sc across – 19 (20, 21, 23) sc. Repeat last 2 rows 4 (5, 5, 6) times.

For 6 month and 18 month sizes only
Repeat Row 21 (23) once more – 10 (10, 10, 11) sc. Fasten off.

Left Front
Row 20 (21, 22, 22): Sk 29 (31, 32, 33) sc of Row 19 (20, 21, 21) from beg of Right Front and join yarn to next sc; ch 1, sc in same sc, sc to last 2 sc, sc2tog – 21 (22, 23, 25) sc.

Row 21 (22, 23, 23): Ch 1, sk first sc, sc in each sc across – 20 (21, 22, 24) sc.

Row 22 (23, 24, 24): Ch 1, sc in each sc to last 2 sc, sc2tog – 19 (20, 21, 23) sc. Continue as for Right Front, reversing shaping. Fasten off.

Back
Row 1: Join yarn with sl st to next free sc after Right Front, ch 1, sc in same st, sc across next 28 (30, 31, 32) sc to edge of Left Front. Turn.

Rows 2-12 (2-13, 2-14, 2-15): Ch 1, sc in each sc. Fasten off.

SLEEVES (make 2)
Ch 26 (28, 30, 31).

Row 1: Sc in 2nd ch from hook and in each ch across – 25 (27, 29, 30) sc. Turn.

Row 2: Ch 1, sc in each sc across. Turn each row.

Row 3 (Dec Row): Ch 1, sc in first 2 sc, sc2tog, sc in each sc to last 4 sc, sc2tog, sc in last 2 sc – 23 (25, 27, 28) sc.

Rows 4-6: Work even in sc.

Row 7: Repeat Row 3.

Continue as established, working Dec Row every 4 rows 2 (3, 3, 3) times more – 17 (17, 19, 20) sc.

Work even for 3 (0, 2, 4) rows. Fasten off.

Continued on page 23.

GUMDROP BABY HAT

DESIGNER: KIM KOTARY

■□□□ EASY

Finished Size: (S/0-12 months) and (M/12-24 months) 14" [35.5 cm] and (16" [40.5 cm]) circumference

MATERIALS
■ LION BRAND® Microspun Microfiber Sport Weight Yarn
[2¹⁄₂ ounces, 168 yd (70 grams, 154 meters) per ball]
1 ball #100 Lily White (A)
1 ball #146 Fuchsia (B)
1 ball #194 Lime (C)
1 ball #148 Turquoise (D)
or colors of your choice
■ LION BRAND size I-9 [5.5 mm] crochet hook or size needed for gauge
■ LION BRAND large-eyed blunt needle
■ LION BRAND split ring marker

GAUGE
16 sc and 18 rows = 4" [10 cm]

HAT
With A and leaving a long tail, ch 4, sl st in first ch to form a ring. Ch 1.

Rnd 1: 8 sc in ring.

Mark beg of rnd and move marker each rnd.

Rnd 2: 2 sc in each sc – 16 sts.

Rnd 3: * 1 sc in next sc, 2 sc in next sc; rep from * 7 times – 24 sts.

Rnd 4: * 1 sc in next 2 sc, 2 sc in next sc; rep from * 7 times – 32 sts.

Rnd 5: * 1 sc in next 3 sc, 2 sc in next sc; rep from * 7 times – 40 sts.

Rnd 6: * 1 sc in next 4 sc, 2 sc in next sc; rep from * 7 times – 48 sts.

Rnd 7: * 1 sc in next 5 sc, 2 sc in next sc; rep from * 7 times – 56 sts.

For M Size hat only
Rnd 8: * 1 sc in next 6 sc, 2 sc in next sc; rep from * 7 times – 64 sts.

For Both Sizes
Work 25 rnds even in sc.

Next Rnd: Sl st in next sc, ch 3, dc in each sc, sl st in top of ch 3 to join.

Next Rnd: Ch 1, sc in each sc around, sl st in beg ch to join. Repeat last rnd once. Fasten off. Weave in ends.

With long tail at beg of Rnd 1, ch 8. Fasten off. Fold ch in half to form a loop and sew to top of hat.

Bobbles (make 24 total – 8 each from B, C, and D)
Ch 4. Yo, insert hook into 4th ch from hook and draw up a loop, yo and draw through 2 loops. (Yo twice, insert hook into same ch and draw up a loop. Yo, draw through 2 loops) 3 times. Yo, insert hook into same ch and draw up a loop, yo and draw through 2 loops. Yo and draw through all loops on hook, ch 4, sl st in beg ch. Fasten off, leaving a long tail to sew Bobble onto hat.

Sew one row of Bobbles 2 rnds below last rnd of incs. Mixing colors as desired, sew 2 more evenly spaced rows of Bobbles.

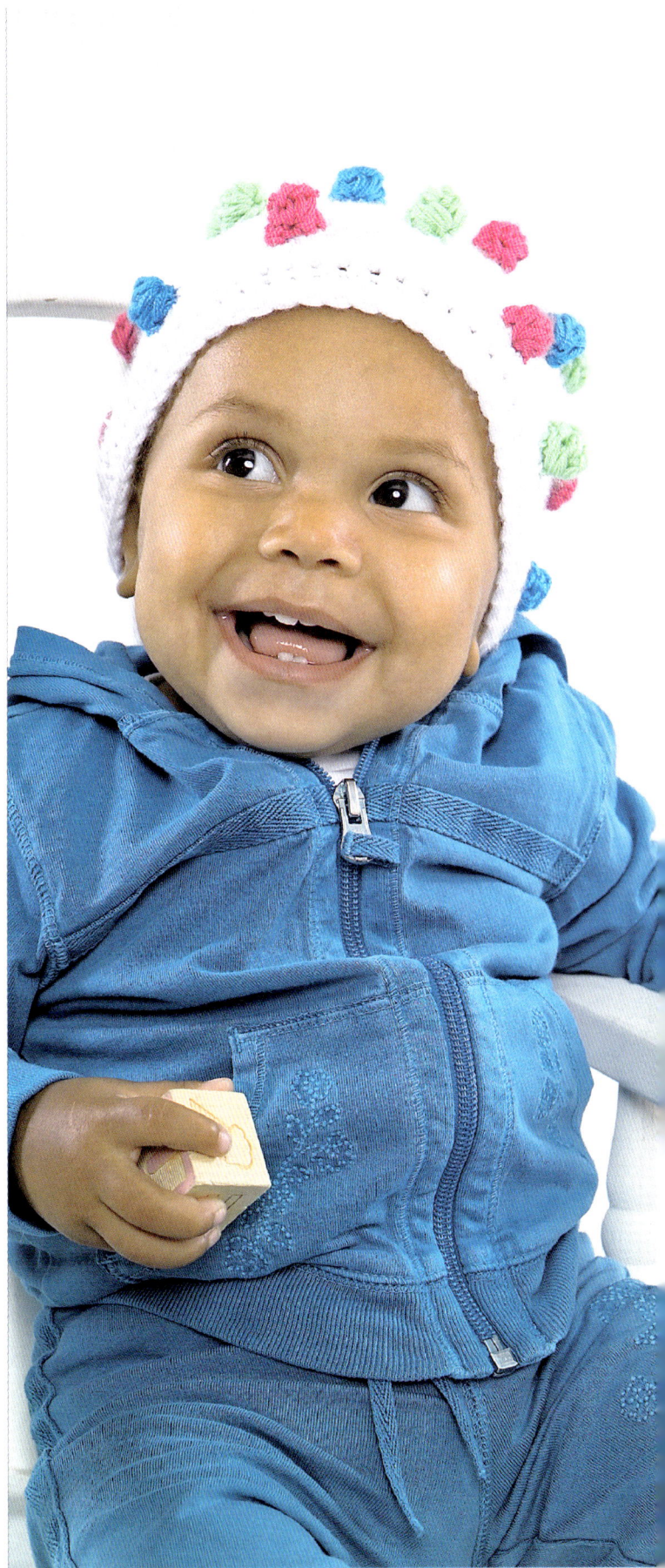

KITTY BLANKIE

DESIGNER: LINDA CYR

EASY

Finished Size: 21" [53.5 cm] square

MATERIALS
- LION BRAND® Microspun Microfiber **3** LIGHT
  Sport Weight Yarn
  [2½ ounces, 168 yd (70 grams, 154 meters)
  per ball
  2 balls #098 French Vanilla (A)
  3 balls #144 Lilac (B)
  1 ball #124 Mocha (C)
  1 ball #186 Mango (D)
  or colors of your choice
- LION BRAND size J-10 [6 mm] crochet hook or
  size needed for gauge
- LION BRAND large-eyed blunt needle
- LION BRAND split ring marker
- Polyester fiberfill stuffing

GAUGE
12 sc and 14 rows = 4" [10 cm] with 2 strands
held tog

BLANKIE
With 2 strands of A held together, ch 40.

Row 1: Sc in 2nd ch from hook and in each ch
across – 39 sc. Ch 1, turn.

Row 2: Sc across.

Repeat Row 2 until piece measures 13" [33 cm]
from beginning. DO NOT TURN.

Border

Rnd 1: With RS facing, turn piece and work 39 sc along left edge of piece, work 2 more sc in last st (counts as corner and first st of next side), work 38 sc along bottom edge, work 2 more sc in last st, work 38 sc along right edge, work 2 more sc in last st, work 38 sc along top edge, work 1 more sc in last st (corner) – 160 sts (39 sts along each side and 1 st in each corner). Place marker for beg of rnd. Sl marker each rnd. Fasten off A and join 2 strands of B.

Rnd 2: Ch 1, (sc to corner, 3 sc in corner) 4 times, sc to marker, sl st to beg ch to join.

Repeat last rnd 12 more times. Fasten off.

POCKET

With 2 strands of C held tog, ch 31.

Row 1: Sc in 2nd ch from hook and in each ch across – 30 sc. Ch 1, turn.

Row 2: Sc in each sc.

Repeat Row 2 until piece measures 8" [20.5 cm] from beg. Fasten off.

FINISHING

Position Pocket 2½" [6.5 cm] from side edges and 1½" [4 cm] from bottom edge of A square. Sew Pocket along sides and bottom edges. Weave in ends.

KITTY
LEGS (make 2)

With 2 strands of D held together, ch 12.

Rnd 1: Sc in first ch to form a ring, sc in each ch – 12 sts. Place marker for beg of rnd. Sl marker each rnd.

Repeat last rnd 7 more times. Sl st to beg sc to join, fasten off. Repeat to make second Leg but do not fasten off.

BODY

Rnd 1: Work 6 sc across second Leg, ch 2, work 12 sc around first Leg, ch 2, work 6 sc from second leg – 24 sc. Place marker for beg of rnd. Sl marker each rnd.

Rnd 2: Sc in next 6 sc, (insert hook into ch and through bottom of opposite ch, sc through both sts to join) twice, sc in next 12 sc, (insert hook into ch and through bottom of opposite ch, sc to join) twice, sc in next 6 sc – 28 sts.

Work even until piece measures 8" (20.5 cm) from beg of Leg. Fasten off.

Continued on page 23.

WEE SHRUG
DESIGNER: **DREW EMBORSKY**

◖■■■▷ EXPERIENCED

Finished Size: 0-6 months (12-24 months)
Finished Circumference: 17$\frac{1}{2}$ (20)" [44.5 (51) cm]
Finished Length: 6 (8)" [15.25 (20.25) cm]
Note: Pattern is written for smaller size with changes for larger size in parentheses. When only one number is given, it applies to both sizes. To follow pattern more easily, circle all numbers pertaining to your size before beginning.

MATERIALS

LIGHT
3

- LION BRAND® Microspun Microfiber
  Sport Weight Yarn
  [2$\frac{1}{2}$ ounces, 168 yards (70 grams, 154 meters) per ball]
  1 (2) ball(s) #186 Mango (A)
  1 (1) ball #103 Coral (B)
  or colors of your choice
- LION BRAND size H-8 [5 mm] crochet hook or size needed for gauge
- LION BRAND large-eyed blunt needle
- LION BRAND split ring markers

GAUGE
19 dc and 8 rows = 4" [10 cm]

BODY
With A, ch 68 (80).

Row 1 (RS): Sc in 2nd ch from hook and in each ch across – 67 (79) sc. Mark this row as RS. Turn each row.

Row 2: Ch 3 (counts as first dc), dc in 2 sc, * ch 1, sk 1 sc, dc in 3 sc; rep from * across – 16 (19) sps.

Row 3: Ch 5, 3 dc in next ch-1 sp, * ch 1, 3 dc in next ch-1 sp; rep from * across, ch 3, dc in top ch-3.

Row 4: Ch 3, 2 dc in next sp, * ch 1, 3 dc in next sp; rep from * across.

Repeat last 2 rows 1 (2) time(s). Fasten off.

BACK
From RS, join A in 4th (5th) ch-sp from right edge.

Row 1: Ch 3, 2 dc in same sp, * ch 1, 3 dc in next sp; rep from * 8 (9) times. Turn each row.

Row 2: Ch 5, 3 dc in next sp, * ch 1, 3 dc in next sp; rep from * across, ch 3, dc in top of ch-3.

Row 3: Ch 3, 2 dc in next sp, * ch 1, 3 dc in next sp; rep from * across.

Repeat last 2 rows 1 (2) times, then Row 2 once more. Fasten off.

RIGHT FRONT
From RS, join A to first dc at right edge.

Row 1: Ch 5, 3 dc in next sp, [ch 1, 3 dc in next sp] 0 (1) time, ch 2, sk 2 dc, dc in next dc. Turn each row.

Row 2: Ch 3, 2 dc in same sp, [ch 1, 3 dc in next sp] 1 (2) times.

Row 3: Ch 5, 3 dc in next sp, [ch 1, 3 dc in next sp] 0 (1) time, ch 2, sk 2 dc, dc in next dc.

Repeat last 2 rows 1 (2) times, then Row 2 once more. Fasten off.

Right Front Extension
From RS, working along front edge, join A with a sl st to first (third) sp from bottom.

Row 1: Ch 3, 2 dc in same sp, * ch 1, 3 dc in next sp; rep from * across – 4 ch-1 sps. Turn each row.

Row 2: Ch 1, sl st in first 3 sts and into sp, ch 3, 2 dc in same sp, * ch 1, 3 dc in next sp; rep from * once.

Row 3: Ch 1, sl st in first 3 sts and into sp, ch 3, 2 dc in same sp, ch 1, 3 dc in next sp.

Row 4: Ch 1, sl st in first 3 sts and into sp, ch 3, 2 dc in same sp. Fasten off.

From WS, join A with a sc in the bottom corner (4th row) of Back, * ch 2, sc in corner st of the next row of Right Front Extension; rep from * 4 more times, 2 sc in next st, sc in next st *. Rep from * to * 4 more times. Fasten off.

LEFT FRONT
From RS, sk 2 sps to left of Back, join A with a sl st to next st.

Row 1: Ch 5, 3 dc in next sp, [ch 1, 3 dc in next sp] 0 (1) time, ch 2, sk 2 dc, dc in top of ch-3.

Row 2: Ch 3, turn, 2 dc in same st, [ch 1, 3 dc in next sp] 1 (2) times.

Row 3: Ch 5, turn, 3 dc in next sp, [ch 1, 3 dc in next sp] 0 (1) time, ch 2, sk 2 st, dc in top of ch-3.

Repeat last 2 rows 1 (2) time(s), then Row 2 once more. Fasten off.

Left Front Extension
From RS, working along front edge of Left Front, join A with a sl st to first (third) sp. Work Left Front Extension as for Right Front Extension, reversing shaping. Sew shoulder seams.

Continued on page 24.

FELTED BABY BOOTIES

DESIGNER: **EDIE ECKMAN**

◼◼◻◻ EASY +

Finished Sizes: 3-6 (6-9, 12-18, 18-24) months

Finished Lengths: About 4$\frac{1}{2}$ (5, 5$\frac{1}{2}$, 6)" [11.5 (12.5, 14, 15) cm] after felting

Note: Pattern is written for smallest size with changes for larger sizes in parentheses. When only one number is given, it applies to all sizes. To follow pattern more easily, circle all numbers pertaining to your size before beginning.

MATERIALS
White Booties
◼ LION BRAND® Lion® Wool Worsted Weight 100% Wool Yarn

MEDIUM 4

[Solid colors: 3 ounces, 158 yards (85 grams, 144 meters); Prints: 2$\frac{3}{4}$ ounces, 143 yards (78 grams, 131 meters) per ball]
1 ball #099 Winter White (A)
or color of your choice

◼ LION BRAND® Tiffany Sport Weight Yarn

LIGHT 3

[1$\frac{3}{4}$ ounces, 137 yards (50 grams, 125 meters) per ball]
1 ball #098 Cream (B)
or color of your choice

◼ 1 (1$\frac{1}{2}$, 2, 2)" [2.5 (4, 5, 5) cm] square of cardboard

Black Booties
◼ LION BRAND® Lion® Wool Worsted Weight Yarn

MEDIUM 4

[Solid colors: 3 ounces, 158 yards (85 grams, 144 meters); Prints: 2$\frac{3}{4}$ ounces, 143 yards (78 grams, 131 meters) per ball]
1 ball #153 Ebony (A)
Small amount #140 Rose (B)
Small amount #099 Winter White (C)
or colors of your choice
◼ Embroidery needle

Mary Jane Booties

MEDIUM 4

◼ LION BRAND® Lion® Wool Worsted Weight Yarn
[Solid colors: 3 ounces, 158 yards (85 grams, 144 meters); Prints: 2$\frac{3}{4}$ ounces, 143 yards (78 grams, 131 meters) per ball]
1 ball #140 Rose (A)
or color of your choice
◼ 2 small snaps
◼ Sewing needle and matching thread

All Booties
◼ LION BRAND crochet hook size K-10.5 [6.5 mm] or size needed for gauge
◼ LION BRAND split ring marker
◼ LION BRAND large-eyed blunt needle

GAUGE
11 sc and 12 rows = 4" [10 cm] with A before felting

STITCH EXPLANATIONS

sc2tog (sc dec): Insert hook into st and draw up a lp. Insert hook into next st and draw up a lp. Yo, draw through all 3 lps on hook.
hdc2tog (hdc dec): (Yo, insert hook into next st and draw up a lp) twice, yo and draw through all 5 lps on hook.

WHITE BOOTIE

With A, ch 8 (9, 10, 11).

Rnd 1 (RS): 3 sc in 2nd ch from hook, sc in 5 (6, 7, 8) ch, 3 sc in last ch; working along opposite side of foundation ch, sc in 5 (6, 7, 8) ch – 16 (18, 20, 22) sc. Place marker at end of rnd, but do not join.

Rnd 2: *2 sc in each of next 3 sc, sc in 5 (6, 7, 8) sc; rep from * once – 22 (24, 26, 28) sc.

Rnd 3: Sc in next sc, (2 sc in next sc) 4 times, sc in 8 (9, 10, 11) sc, (2 sc in next sc) twice, sc in 7 (8, 9, 10) sc – 28 (30, 32, 34) sc.

Rnd 4: (Sc in next sc, 2 sc in next sc) 4 times, sc in 10 (11, 12, 13) sc, (2 sc in next sc) twice, sc in 8 (9, 10, 11) sc – 34 (36, 38, 40) sc.

Rnd 5: Sc in next 5 sc, (2 sc in next sc) 4 times, sc in 13 (14, 15, 16) sc, 2 sc in next sc, sc in next 2 sc, 2 sc in next sc, sc in 8 (9, 10, 11) sc – 40 (42, 44, 46) sc.

Rnd 6: Sc through back lp of each sc around.

Rnd 7: Sc in next 4 sc, hdc in next 2 sc, dc in next
6 sc, hdc in next 2 sc, sc to end of rnd.

Rnd 8: Sc in next 2 sc, sc2tog, hdc2tog, hdc in next dc, (hdc2tog) twice, hdc in next dc, hdc2tog, sc2tog, sc to end of rnd – 34 (36, 38, 40) sts.

Rnd 9: Sc in next 4 sts, hdc in next 4 sts, sc to end of rnd.

Rnd 10: Sc in next 4 sc, (sc2tog) twice, sc to end of rnd – 32 (34, 36, 38) sc.

Rnd 11: (Sc2tog) 5 times, sc to end of rnd – 27 (29, 31, 33) sc.

Rnd 12: Sc2tog, sc in next sc, sc2tog, sc to end of rnd – 25 (27, 29, 31) sc.

Sizes 6-9, 12-18, and 18-24 months only
Rnd 13: (Sc2tog) twice, sc to end of rnd -- (25, 27, 29) sc.

Sizes 12-18 and 18-24 months only
Rnd 14: Rep Rnd 13 -- (25, 27) sc.

All Sizes
Next Rnd: Sc in each sc around -- 25 (25, 25, 27) sc.
Work 3 more rnds even in sc. Fasten off.
With RS facing, join A at back heel on Rnd 6. Ch 1, sc into remaining lp of each sc around Rnd 6; join with sl st to beg sc. Fasten off.
Weave in ends.

Continued on page 24.

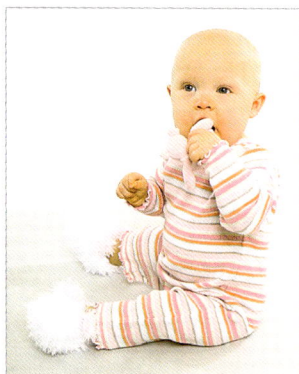

BUNNY SLIPPERS

DESIGNER: MICHELE THOMPSON

⬤⬛☐☐ EASY

Finished Sizes: S (M, L, XL)
Foot Length: About $4^1/_2$ (5, $5^1/_2$, $5^3/_4$)"
[11.5 (13, 14, 14.5) cm]
Finished Length: $4^3/_4$ ($5^1/_4$, $5^3/_4$, 6)"
12 (13.5, 14.5, 15) cm]
Note: Pattern is written for smallest size with changes for larger sizes in parentheses. When only one number is given, it applies to all sizes. To follow pattern more easily, circle all numbers pertaining to your size before beginning.

MATERIALS

■ LION BRAND® Tiffany Sport Weight Yarn ⟨3 LIGHT⟩
   [$1^3/_4$ ounces, 137 yards (50 grams, 125 meters) per ball]
   1 (2, 2, 2) ball(s) # 100 White (A)
   1 ball #101 Soft Pink (B)
   or colors of your choice
■ LION BRAND crochet hook size K-10.5 [6.5 mm]
   or size needed for gauge
■ LION BRAND large-eyed blunt needle

GAUGE

14 sc and 13 rows = 4" [10 cm] with 2 strands of A held tog

STITCH EXPLANATION

sc2tog (sc dec): Insert hook into st and draw up a loop. Insert hook into next st and draw up a loop. Yarn over, draw through all 3 loops on hook.

SLIPPERS

With 2 strands of A held tog, ch 19 (21, 21, 23).

Row 1: Sc in 2nd from hook and in each ch across – 18 (20, 20, 22) sc. Turn.

Rows 2-13 (2-15, 2-17, 2-18): Ch 1, sc in each sc across. Turn each row.

Row 14 (16, 18, 19): (Sc2tog) across – 9 (10, 10, 11) sc.

Row 15 (17, 19, 20): Ch 1, sc in each st across. Fasten off, leaving a long tail.

FINISHING

Fold piece in half lengthwise and sew back seam. With large-eyed blunt needle, weave long tail through top loops of last row of sc, pull tightly, and fasten securely. Sew top seam to within 2½" [6.5 cm] of back seam.

Ears (make 4)

With 2 strands of B held tog, ch 6.

Row 1: Sl st in 2nd ch from hook, sc in next ch, hdc in next 3 ch. Fasten off, leaving a long tail.

Sew 2 Ears to front of each Slipper.

STUFFED DOLL

DESIGNER: **PEGGY GREIG**

■●□□ **EASY +**

Finished Size: About 9" [23 cm] tall

MATERIALS
- LION BRAND® Microspun Microfiber Sport **LIGHT 3** Weight Yarn
  2½ ounces, 168 yards (70 grams, 154 meters) per ball]
  1 ball #158 Buttercup (A)
  1 ball #148 Turquoise (B)
  1 ball #143 Lavender (C)
  1 ball #194 Lime (D)
  1 ball #186 Mango (E)
  or colors of your choice
- LION BRAND crochet hook size G-6 [4 mm] or size needed for gauge
- LION BRAND split ring markers
- LION BRAND large-eyed blunt needle
- Fiberfill stuffing
- Embroidery floss in light brown, dark brown and red
- Embroidery needle
- 3" [7.5 cm] square of cardboard

GAUGE
18 sc and 20 rows = 4" [10 cm]

STITCH EXPLANATION
sc2tog (sc decrease): Insert hook into st and draw up a loop. Insert hook into next st and draw up a loop. Yarn over, draw through all 3 loops on hook.

DOLL

With A, ch 2, work 4 sc in 2nd ch from hook; join with sl st in beg sc. Place marker for beg of rnd.
Sl marker each rnd.

Rnds 1 and 2: Ch 1, 2 sc in each sc around; join with sl st in beg sc – 16 sc at end of Rnd 2.

Rnd 3: Ch 1, *2 sc in next sc, sc in next sc; rep from * around; join with sl st in beg sc – 24 sc.

Rnd 4: Ch 1, *2 sc in next sc, sc in next 2 sc; rep from * around; join with sl st in beg sc – 32 sc.

Rnds 5-14: With A, ch 1, sc in each sc around; join with sl st in beg sc.

Rnds 15 and 16: With B, rep Rnd 5.

Rnds 17-19: With C, rep Rnd 5.

Rnds 20-23: With D, rep Rnd 5.

Rnds 24 and 25: With E, rep Rnd 5.

Rnds 26-30: With B, rep Rnd 5.

Rnd 31: With C, rep Rnd 5.

Rnds 32-34: With D, rep Rnd 5.

Rnds 35-38: With E, rep Rnd 5.

Rnds 39-41: With B, rep Rnd 5.

Stuff Doll.

Rnd 42: With C, ch 1, *sc2tog in next 2 sc, sc in next 2 sc; rep from * around; join with sl st in first sc – 24 sc.

Rnd 43: Ch 1, *sc2tog in next 2 sc, sc in next sc; rep from * around; join with sl st in beg sc – 16 sc.

Rnds 44-46: Ch 1, (sc2tog in next 2 sc) around; join with sl st in first sc – 2 sc at end of Rnd 46.

Fasten off.

FINISHING

Weave in ends. With light brown floss and embroidery needle and using photograph as a guide for placement, embroider eyes with satin sts. With red floss, embroider mouth with straight sts. With dark brown floss, embroider 2 curved lines of running sts through both layers and stuffing, along each side of Body to create arms.

Continued on page 20.

STUFFED DOLL
CONTINUED FROM PAGE 19

ROLL BRIM HAT

Beg at top of Hat, with D, ch 2, work 4 sc in 2nd ch from hook; join with sl st in first sc. Place marker for beg of rnd. Sl marker each rnd.

Rnds 1 and 2: Ch 1, 2 sc in each sc around; join with sl st in beg sc – 16 sc at end of Rnd 2.

Rnd 3: Ch 1, *2 sc in next sc, sc in next sc; rep from * around; join with sl st in beg sc – 24 sc.

Rnd 4: Ch 1, *2 sc in next sc, sc in next 2 sc; rep from * around; join with sl st in beg sc – 32 sc.

Rnds 5-10: Ch 1, sc in each sc around; join with sl st in beg sc.

Drop D; join E.

Rnd 11: Ch 1, sc in each sc around; join with sl st in beg sc.

Rnd 12: Ch 1, *2 sc in next sc, sc in next 3 sc; rep from * around; join with sl st in beg sc – 40 sc.

Rnd 13: Ch 1, *2 sc in next sc, sc in next 4 sc; rep from * around; join with sl st in beg sc – 48 sc.

Rnds 14 and 15: Ch 1, sc in each sc around; join with sl st in beg sc.

Fasten off.

TASSEL

Wrap E around 3" [7.5 cm] square of cardboard 34 times. Cut 2 lengths of E each 8" [20.5 cm] and thread, doubled, into large-eyed blunt needle. Insert needle under all strands at upper edge of cardboard. Pull tightly and knot securely near strands. Cut yarn loops at lower edge of cardboard. Cut an 8" [20.5 cm] length of D and wrap tightly around loops 1" [2.5 cm] below topknot to form Tassel neck. Knot securely; thread ends onto needle and weave ends to center of Tassel. Trim Tassel ends evenly. Sew Tassel to top of Hat.

POINTED HAT

Beg at top of Hat, with E, ch 2, work 4 sc in 2nd ch from hook; join with sl st in first sc. Place marker for beg of rnd. Sl marker each rnd.

Rnd 1: Ch 1, 2 sc in each sc around; join with sl st in beg sc – 8 sc.

Rnds 2-4: Ch 1, sc in each sc around; join with sl st in beg sc.

Rnds 5-8: Rep Rnds 1-4 – 16 sc.

Rnd 9: Ch 1, *2 sc in next sc, sc in next sc; rep from * around; join with sl st in beg sc – 24 sc.

Rnds 10-12: Ch 1, sc in each sc around; join with sl st in first sc.

Rnd 13: Ch 1, *2 sc in next sc, sc in next 2 sc; rep from * around; join with sl st in beg sc – 32 sc.

Rnds 14-16: Ch 1, sc in each sc around; join with sl st in beg sc.

Drop E; join B.

Rnds 17-22: Ch 1, sc in each sc around; join with sl st in beg sc.
Fasten off.

TASSEL

With B, work as for Tassel of Roll Brim Hat, using E to tie Tassel. Sew Tassel to point of Hat.

STRIPED BABY HAT
CONTINUED FROM PAGE 3

Row 6: Ch 1, sc in 5 sc. Fasten off but do not cut yarn.

Row 7: Attach 2 strands of A with sl st in first st, ch 1, sc in 4 sc.

Row 8: Ch 1, sc in 3 sc. Fasten off but do not cut yarn.

TIE
Ch to desired length with each color. Braid chs tog for Tie.

LEFT EAR FLAP
Sk 16 (20) sc across front and work Left Ear Flap and Tie same as Right Ear Flap and Tie.

TASSEL
Wrap strands of each color yarn around 2" [5 cm] cardboard. Cut an 8" [20.5 cm] length of yarn and thread, doubled, onto large-eyed blunt needle. Insert needle under all strands at one edge of cardboard. Pull tightly and knot securely near strands. Cut yarn loops at opposite edge of cardboard. Cut a 10" [25.5 cm] length of yarn and wrap tightly around loops 1" [2.5 cm] below topknot to form Tassel neck. Knot securely; thread ends into needle and weave ends to center of Tassel. Trim Tassel ends evenly. Sew Tassel to end of Tie.

FINISHING
Attach 2 strands of B with sl st at center back. Sc in each sc to Ear Flap, ✝ sc along edge of Ear Flap, work 2 sc at tip of Flap, sc along opposite edge of Ear Flap ✝, sc in each sc to second Ear Flap, rep from ✝ to ✝, sc in each sc to end of rnd, sl st in first sc to join. Fasten off. Weave in ends.

CROCHET TEDDY BEAR
CONTINUED FROM PAGE 5

Rnd 15: Ch 1, * sc in 3 sc, 2 sc in next sc; rep from * around – 40 sc.

Rnds 16 and 17: Ch 1, sc in each sc around.

Shape Armholes
Rnd 18: Ch 1, sc in 9 sc, sk 8 sc, sc in 12 sc, sk 8 sc, sc in 3 sc – 24 sc.

Rnd 19: Ch 1, sc in 12 sc, 2 sc in next sc, sc in 4 sc, 2 sc in next sc, sc in 6 sc – 26 sc.

Rnd 20: Ch 1, sc in 14 sc, 2 sc in next sc, sc in 2 sc, 2 sc in next sc, sc in 8 sc – 28 sc.

Rnds 21-23: Ch 1, sc in each sc around.

Rnd 24: Ch 1, sc in 10 sc, * sc2tog, sc in 4 sc, sc2tog; rep from * once, sc in 2 sc – 24 sc.

Rnd 25: Ch 1, sc in 13 sc, sc2tog, sc in 4 sc, sc2tog, sc in 3 sc – 22 sc.

Rnd 26: Ch 1, sc in 8 sc, sc2tog, * sc in 2 sc, sc2tog; rep from * twice – 18 sc.

Rnd 27: Ch 1, * sc2tog; rep from * around – 9 sc.

Fasten off leaving an 8" [20.5 cm] tail. Stuff Body. Weave yarn tail through sts of final rnd and pull tightly to close.

ARMS

From RS, join yarn at one underarm and work 10 sc evenly around armhole. Place marker for beg of rnd. Sl marker each rnd.

Rnds 1-9: Ch 1, sc in each sc around, sl st in first sc to join each rnd.

Fasten off leaving an 8" [20.5 cm] tail. Stuff Arm. Weave tail through sts of final rnd and pull tightly to close. Repeat for second Arm.

LEGS (make 2)

Note: To shape Legs, count odd rnds as RS for left Leg, as WS for right Leg.

Beg at sole of foot, ch 4.

Rnd 1 (RS for left leg, WS for right leg): 2 sc into 2nd ch from hook, sc in next ch, 2 sc in last ch, working along opposite side of ch, 2 sc in same ch, sc in next ch, 2 sc in last ch, sl st in first sc to join each rnd – 10 sc. Place marker for beg of rnd. Sl marker each rnd.

Rnd 2: Ch 1, * 2 sc in next sc, sc in 3 sc, 2 sc in next sc; rep from * once – 14 sc.

Rnd 3: Ch 1, sc in each sc around.

Rnd 4: Ch 1, sc in 5 sc, (sc2tog) twice, sc in 5 sc – 12 sc.

Rnd 5: Ch 1, sc in 4 sc, (sc2tog) twice, sc in 4 sc – 10 sc.

Rnds 6-12: Ch 1, sc in each sc around.

Shape Hip
Row 13: Ch 1, sc in 5 sc, sc2tog, DO NOT JOIN – 6 sc. Turn each row.

Row 14: Ch 1, sc in 4 sc, sc2tog – 5 sc.

Row 15: Ch 1, sc in 3 sc, sc2tog – 4 sc.

Row 16: Ch 1, sc in 2 sc, sc2tog – 3 sc.

Fasten off. Stuff legs and sew to body.

EARS (make 2)

Rnd 1: Beg with slipknot, leaving a 6" [15 cm] yarn tail, work 8 sc in sl st; sl st in first sc to join each rnd. After working the first round, pull gently on the yarn tail to close ring.

Rnd 2: Ch 1, sc in 7 sc, 2 sc in last sc – 9 sc.

Rnd 3: Ch 1, sc in each sc around. Fasten off. Flatten and gently curve Ear. Sew in place.

FINISHING

With black yarn and large-eyed needle, following Diagram and using photograph as a guide for placement, embroider eyes, nose, and mouth with straight sts. Weave in ends.

DIAGRAM

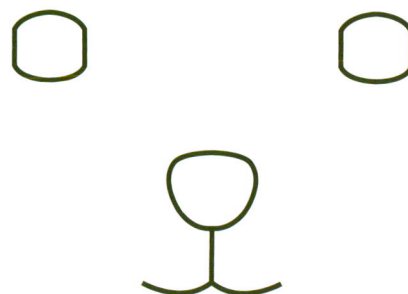

SCARF

With Microspun yarn and smaller hook, ch 65.

Row 1: Sc in second ch from hook; sc in each ch across – 64 sc.

Row 2: Ch 1, turn; sc in each sc across – 64 sc.

Row 3: Ch 1, turn; sc in each sc across – 64 sc. Fasten off.

CROSS-FRONT BABY SWEATER
CONTINUED FROM PAGE 7

FINISHING
Sew shoulder seams. Sew sleeve seams. Sew in sleeves.

EDGING
From RS, join yarn on lower right front corner. Sc evenly around neck and front edges, working 3 sc in each corner at beg of neck shaping. Fasten off.

SIDE TIES (make 4)
Ch 35, fasten off and weave in ends. Sew a Tie to RS at beg of neck shaping on each Front. Sew remaining Ties on side edges (1 Tie will be inside sweater) to match placement.

FLOWERS (make 3)
Ch 4, sl st in first ch to form a ring.

Rnd 1: Ch 5, * sc in ring, ch 3; rep from * 6 times; join with sl st to 2nd ch of beg ch-5.

Rnd 2: * [Sc, hdc, 3 dc, hdc, sc] in next ch-3 sp; rep from * 6 times; join with sl st to beg sc.

Fasten off.

Weave in ends. Following photograph, sew Flowers to Fronts.

KITTY BLANKIE
CONTINUED FROM PAGE 11

ARMS (make 2)
With 2 strands of D held tog, ch 10.

Rnd 1: Sc in first ch to form a ring, sc in each ch – 10 sts. Place marker for beg of rnd. Sl marker each rnd.

Repeat last rnd 5 more times, sl st in beg sc to join. Fasten off.

EARS (make 2)
With 2 strands of D held tog, ch 2.

Rnd 1: Work 3 sc in 2nd ch from hook.

Rnd 2: Inc 1 st in each st – 6 sts.

Rnd 3: (Sc, inc next st) 3 times – 9 sts.

Rnd 4: (2 sc, inc in next st) 3 times – 12 sts.

Rnd 5: (3 sc, inc in next st) 3 times – 15 sts. Fasten off.

FINISHING
Stuff Legs, then sew ends closed. Stuff Body. Sew top of head closed. Sew ears to head. Sew one end of each Arm closed. Stuff Arms and sew to Body. With one strand of B and large-eyed needle, following diagram and using photograph as a guide for placement, embroider eyes and nose with straight sts and eyes with French knots. Weave in ends.

DIAGRAM

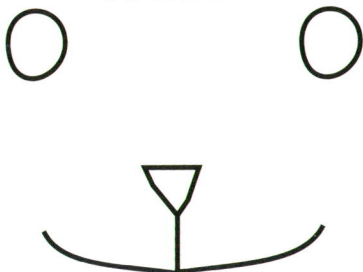

WEE SHRUG

CONTINUED FROM PAGE 13

SLEEVES

From RS, join A with a sl st in any sp along armhole edge.

Rnd 1: Ch 3, 2 dc in same sp, ch 1, * 3 dc in next sp, ch 1; rep from * around, sl st in top of ch-3. Place marker for beg of rnd. Sl marker each rnd.

Rnd 2: Sl st in next two sts and in next sp, ch 3, 2 dc in same sp, ch 1, * 3 dc in next sp, ch 1; rep from * around, sl st in top of ch-3.

Rnds 3-10 (3-14): Repeat Rnd 2.

Rnd 11 (15): Ch 1, sc in same st, sc in each st and sp around, sl st in first sc to join. Fasten off.

Rnd 12 (16): From RS, join B with a sc in any st, ch 3, dc in next st, * sc in next st, ch 3, dc in next st; rep from * around, sl st in first sc to join. Fasten off.

FELTED BABY BOOTIES

CONTINUED FROM PAGE 15

FELTING

Wash by machine on a hot wash/cold rinse cycle with detergent and several pieces of clothing to agitate. To felt additionally, dry by machine on a regular setting until almost dry. Remove from dryer and pull into shape.

POM POM

With B, wrap yarn around cardboard – the more wraps, the fuller the Pompom will be. Cut yarn leading to skein and carefully slide yarn off cardboard. Cut a long piece of yarn and double it; carefully slide it under the center of the yarn and tie tightly with a double knot. Clip the loops, fluff out Pompom, and trim. Use the ends of the knotted strand to attach Pom Pom.

BLACK BOOTIE

With A, work as for White Bootie.

TIES (make 2)

With B, ch 52.

Row 1: Sc in 2nd ch from hook, ch 3, dc in next st, * sc in next st, ch 3, dc in next st; rep from * across. Fasten off.

FINISHING

Weave in ends.

EDGING

Rnd 1: From RS, join A with a sc in any st along the lower edge of Back. Sc evenly around entire outside edge, sl st in first sc to join. Fasten off.

Rnd 2: From RS, join B with a sc in any st along the lower edge of Back. Ch 3, dc in next st, * sc in next st, ch 3, dc in next st; rep from * around, sl st in first sc to join. Fasten off.

Sew Ties to front points of Front Extensions.

FINISHING

Felt Booties. Using photo as a guide, with B, embroider flowers in Lazy Daisy stitch. With C, work French knots for flower centers.

MARY JANE BOOTIE

With A, work as for White Bootie through Rnd 11 (12, 12, 12). Fasten off.

With RS facing, join A at back heel on Rnd 6. Ch 1, sc into remaining lp of each sc around Rnd 6; join with sl st to beg sc. Fasten off.

STRAP (make 2)

With A, ch 14 (15, 16, 17). Hdc in 2nd ch from hook and in each ch across. Fasten off.

FINISHING

Sew short edge of Strap to inner top edge of Bootie. Felt Booties. Sew snap to Strap and to outer edge of Bootie to fit foot.

GENERAL INSTRUCTIONS

ABBREVIATIONS

beg = begin(ning)
ch = chain
ch-sp = space previously made
cm = centimeters
dc = double crochet
dec = decreas(e)(s)(ing)
hdc = half double crochet
inc = increase(e)(s)(ing)
lp(s) = loop(s)
mm = millimeters
rep = repeat
rnd(s) = round(s)
RS = right side
sc = single crochet
sk = skip
sl = slip
sl st = slip stitch
sp = space
st(s) = stitch(es)
tog = together
WS = wrong side
yo = yarn over

* — When you see an asterisk used within a pattern
   row, the symbol indicates that later you will be
   told to repeat a portion of the instruction. Most
   often the instructions will say, repeat from * so
   many times.

( ) or [ ] — Set off a short number of stitches that are
   repeated or indicated additional information.

† to † — work all instructions from first † to
   second † as many times as specified.

GAUGE

Never underestimate the importance of gauge.
Achieving the correct gauge assures that the
finished size of your piece matches the finished size
given in the pattern.

CHECKING YOUR GAUGE

Work a swatch that is at least 4" (10 cm) square.
Use the suggested hook size and the number of
stitches given. For example, the standard Lion
Brand® Homespun® gauge is: 10 single crochet + 10
rows = 4" (10 cm) on a size K-10½ (6.5 mm) hook.
If your swatch is larger than 4" (10 cm), you need
to work it again using a smaller hook; if it is smaller
than 4" (10 cm), try it with a larger hook. This might
require a swatch or two to get the exact gauge given
in the pattern.

METRICS

As a handy reference, keep in mind that 1 ounce =
approximately 28 grams and 1" = 2.5 centimeters.

TERMS

continue in this way or as established — Once a
pattern is set up (established), the instructions may
tell you to continue in the same way.

fasten off — To end your piece, you need to simply
pull the yarn through the last loop left on the hook.
This keeps the last stitch intact and prevents the
work from unraveling.

right side — Refers to the front of the piece.

work even — This is used to indicate an area worked
as established without increasing or decreasing.

◼◻◻◻ **BEGINNER**	Projects for first-time crocheters using basic stitches. Minimal shaping.
◼◼◻◻ **EASY**	Projects using yarn with basic stitches, repetitive stitch patterns, simple color changes, and simple shaping and finishing.
◼◼◼◻ **INTERMEDIATE**	Projects using a variety of techniques, such as basic lace patterns or color patterns, mid-level shaping and finishing.
◼◼◼◼ **EXPERIENCED**	Projects with intricate stitch patterns, techniques and dimension, such as non-repeating patterns, multi-color techniques, fine threads, small hooks, detailed shaping and refined finishing.

CROCHET TERMINOLOGY

UNITED STATES		INTERNATIONAL
slip stitch (slip st)	=	single crochet (sc)
single crochet (sc)	=	double crochet (dc)
half double crochet (hdc)	=	half treble crochet (htr)
double crochet (dc)	=	treble crochet (tr)
treble crochet (tr)	=	double treble crochet (dtr)
double treble crochet (dtr)	=	triple treble crochet (ttr)
triple treble crochet (tr tr)	=	quadruple treble crochet (qtr)
skip	=	miss

Yarn Weight Symbol & Names	SUPER FINE ①1	FINE ②2	LIGHT ③3	MEDIUM ④4	BULKY ⑤5	SUPER BULKY ⑥6
Type of Yarns in Category	Sock, Fingering Baby	Sport, Baby	DK, Light Worsted	Worsted, Afghan, Aran	Chunky, Craft, Rug	Bulky, Roving
Crochet Gauge Ranges in Single Crochet to 4" (10 cm)	21-32 sts	16-20 sts	12-17 sts	11-14 sts	8-11 sts	5-9 sts
Advised Hook Size Range	B-1 to E-4	E-4 to 7	7 to I-9	I-9 to K-10.5	K-10.5 to M-13	M-13 and larger

CROCHET HOOKS												
U.S.	B-1	C-2	D-3	E-4	F-5	G-6	H-8	I-9	J-10	K-10½	N	P	Q
Metric - mm	2.25	2.75	3.25	3.5	3.75	4	5	5.5	6	6.5	9	10	15

BASIC STITCHES & TECHNIQUES

◼ ZEROS

To consolidate the length of an involved pattern, Zeros are sometimes used so that all sizes can be combined. For example, work 0 (1, 1, 2) more rows in ribbing as established means the first size would do nothing, the second and third sizes would work one more row of ribbing , and the largest size would work two rows of ribbing.

◼ HINTS

As in all pieces, good finishing techniques make a big difference in the quality of the piece. Do not tie knots. Always start a new ball at the beginning of a row, leaving ends long enough to weave in later.

◼ CROCHET STITCH
HALF DOUBLE CROCHET
(abbreviated hdc)

Yo, insert hook in stitch indicated, yo and pull up a loop, yo and draw through all 3 loops on hook *(Fig. 1)*.

Fig. 1

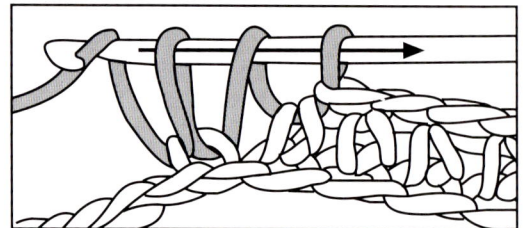

EMBROIDERY STITCHES
FRENCH KNOT

Bring the needle up at 1. Wrap the yarn around the needle once and insert the needle at 2, holding end of yarn with non-stitching fingers *(Fig. 2)*. Tighten knot; then pull needle through, holding the yarn until it must be released.

Fig. 2

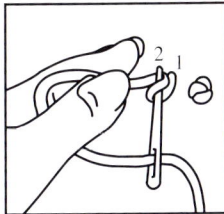

LAZY DAISY STITCH

Thread needle and bring from back to front through crocheted piece (base of petal). *Insert needle as closely as possible to base of petal, then bring needle back up at tip of petal. Loop the yarn under the needle. Pull needle away from you. Insert needle into crocheted piece just over the looped yarn. Take needle to the back to anchor the stitch. Repeat from * for each petal *(Fig. 3)*.

Fig. 3

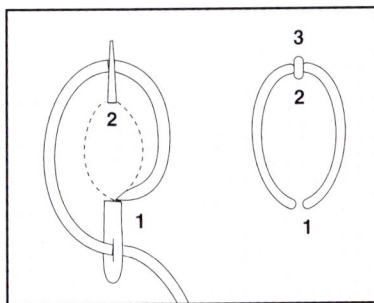

RUNNING STITCH

Thread needle and pass it in and out of the crocheted piece, making the surface stitches and spaces of equal length *(Fig. 4)*.

Fig. 4

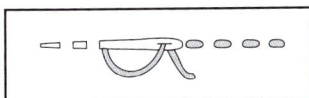

SATIN STITCH

Satin stitch is a series of straight stitches worked side by side so they touch but do not overlap. Come up at odd numbers and go down at even numbers *(Fig. 5)*.

Fig. 5

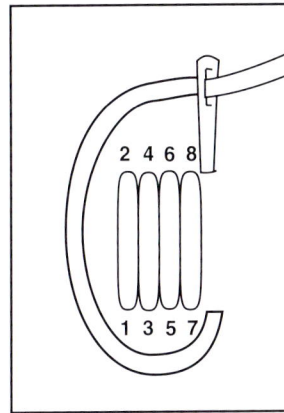

STRAIGHT STITCH

Straight Stitch is just what the name implies, a single, straight stitch. Come up at 1 and go down at 2 *(Fig. 6)*.

Fig. 6

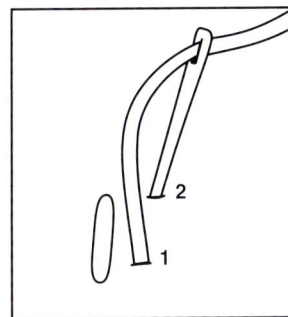

Production Team
Lion Brand Creative Director – *Karen Tanaka*
Lion Brand Managing Editor – *Jean Guirguis*
Lion Brand Fashion Editor – *Stephanie Klose*
Lion Brand Design Editor – *Susan Haviland*
Lion Brand Technical Editor – *Jackie Smyth*
Technical Coordinator – *Mary S. Hutcheson*
Editorial Writer - *Susan Johnson*
Senior Graphic Artist – *Lora Puls*
Photo Stylist - *Angela Alexander*

More Knit and Crochet leaflets featuring
Lion Brand® Yarn!

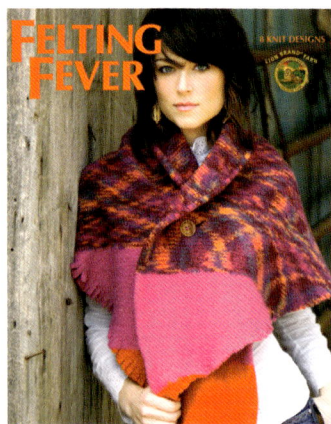

Leaflet 4059

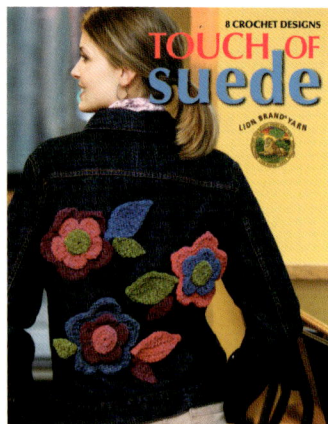

Leaflet 4688

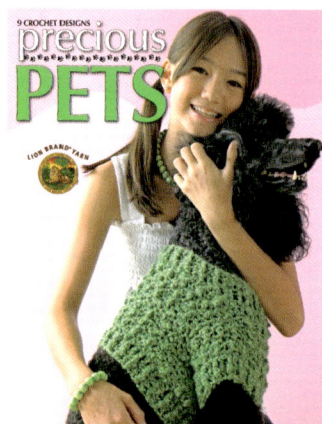

Leaflet 4687

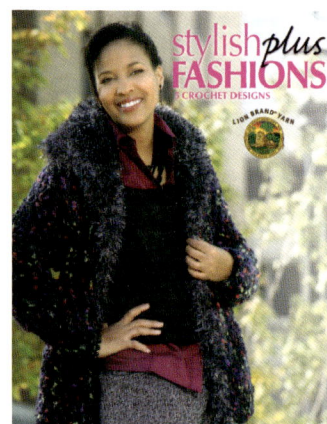

Leaflet 4686

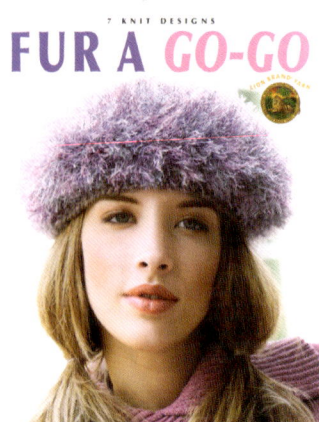

Leaflet 4376

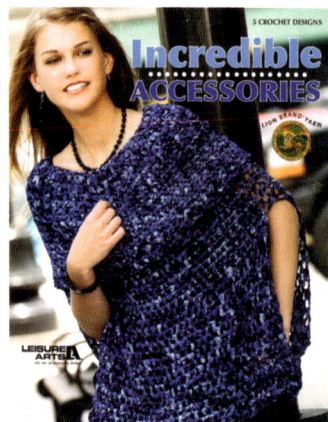

Leaflet 4375

Leaflet 4374

Leaflet 3985

Leaflet 3984

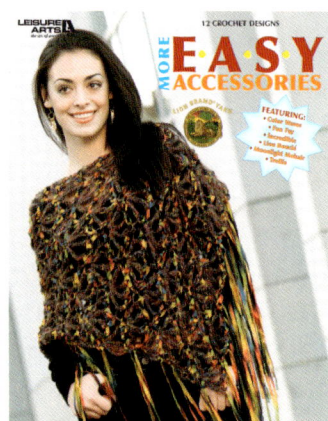

Leaflet 3982

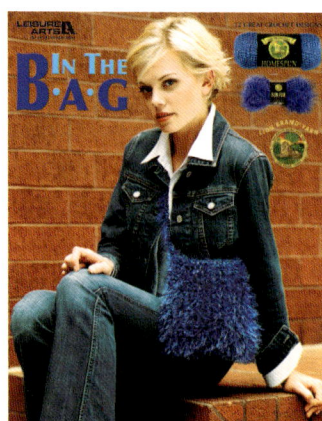

Leaflet 3775

Leaflet 3774

Look for these titles and more at your retailer or visit **www.leisurearts.com**.